A COUPE
OF THORNS
AND ROSÉ

A COUPE OF THORNS AND ROSÉ

Romantasy Cocktails to Quench Your Thirst

CLARKSON POTTER/PUBLISHERS
NEW YORK

Contents

FRUITS OF THE FAE

SCRUMPTIOUS SPRITZES

TOE-CURLING TIPPLES

SERIOUS SPICE AND SLOW BURNERS

Introduction

IT'S ALL ABOUT THE CHEMISTRY

What is it that makes the perfect roman-tasy? And, while we are here, what about the perfect cocktail? Perhaps there's a crossover between the two. Neither should be too sweet or cloying. But neither do we want elements that are eternally at odds—there is such a thing as too much tension! Perhaps it's about balance then, about all the ingredients—cough—coming together to create something that's truly magical.

From martinis to highballs and sours to snappers, it's hard to explain why some cocktails have swept the globe. Maybe we shouldn't try—just like we don't need to understand exactly what it is that makes our toes curl about stories filled with morally gray characters, mythical creatures, and more than a little death. Perhaps the allure is just as instinctual as falling for your mate. And happily, that is what this book is here to do! In these pages you will find 60 cocktails inspired by our favorite romantasy stories. Some may be familiar, some may seem worlds apart from our own, but this is a genre all about discovery. So whether you're into fairies, vampires, demons, or dragons, just like cocktails, there is one out there for everyone.

The greatest romantasy reads take well-loved tropes—enemies to lovers, grumpy vs. sunshine, reverse harems—and make them their own. Sure, the fated couple may have to navigate a few obstacles and warring kingdoms first, but with a generous dose of smut these books create a love so powerful it transcends the page and connects readers everywhere. Is there anything more pleasurable than lighting some candles, curling up in your book nook, and escaping to your favorite realm? Maybe it's adding some extra spice to your book club and sitting down to scream, laugh (or maybe cry!) together about *those* chapters? It could be a date, a group of friends, your BFF (but absolutely not your parents)—introducing them to your favorite series or standalone only enhances the connection. And what better way to set the scene than by making a cocktail to settle down with first?

Whatever you like in a main character—whether you prefer a stabby heroine, a golden retriever pirate captain, or a dark faerie with an *enormous* wingspan—you will find it all on the page. No date can be so awkward, no working day so dull, no night so dark and lonely that a romantasy novel can't make your stomach do somersaults. So let's raise a glass to whatever cocktail piques your interest and make a toast: here's to finding your book boyfriend (or if we're being honest, *boyfriends*). All the cocktails in this recipe book are made for a single serving unless stated otherwise but you can of course multiply up depending on how many you're serving. Glassware is also a suggestion so don't let a lack of specific glassware stop you from having fun!

HOW TO MAKE
YOUR OWN SIMPLE SYRUP

Simple syrup is a common ingredient in this book, so here is an easy guide to making your own. Essentially this is just sugar and water and all the recipes in this book require a mix in the ratio of 1:1 by volume. You can make these easily at home and create a batch so you have it to hand when you fancy a drink.

A 1:1 mix can be made using a blender; just add equal volumes of water and sugar to a blender and blend until well mixed.

To make a 2:1 syrup you will generally need heat to ensure the sugar dissolves in the water. Heat the water gently in a pan, then add half of the sugar. Stir briefly and leave until the mixture becomes clear. Add the remaining sugar and re-peat. Be careful not to over-stir; the mixture will clarify on its own if left, without agitation.

Useful Equipment

Shaker

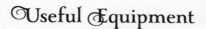

Jigger and measuring spoons/cups

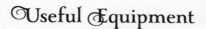

Mixing glass

Barspoon

Strainer

WHAT to SERVE YOUR SHADOW KING

OLD-FASHIONED ALPHA MALE

BRIDE BY ALI HAZELWOOD

Have you found yourself alone with the big, bad wolf? There are only two ways this can go, much the same as this strong yet complex cocktail. So take a sip, settle down with *Bride*, and get ready to go feral.

1 large strip of orange zest, for garnish
⅓ ounce simple syrup or a barspoon of sugar (see Note)
2 or 3 dashes Angostura bitters
1¾ ounces golden or dark rum

Glassware: Rocks glass

Add the strip of orange zest to the bottom of a rocks glass along with the simple syrup, bitters, and half of the rum. Add two cubes of ice and stir 20 to 30 times to mix. Add the remaining rum and two more ice cubes and stir again.

Note: If using sugar, not simple syrup, put the sugar and the bitters into a rocks glass. Add a few drops of rum and stir with a spoon to dissolve the sugar. Add half of the rum to the glass along with two cubes of ice and stir 20 to 30 times to mix. Add the strip of orange zest, the remaining rum, and two more ice cubes before stirring again.

MORALLY GREYHOUND

A COURT THIS CRUEL AND LOVELY
BY STACIA STARK

Completely indifferent to the sweet or sour flavor dichotomy, the Morally Greyhound is the tart cocktail of your dreams. The ambiguity lies in the pink grapefruit juice, which, like everyone's favorite book boyfriend Lorian, has the ability to make you scream for completely opposing reasons. Feel free to use either vodka or gin in this recipe, we really couldn't care less.

2 ounces vodka or gin
7 ounces pink grapefruit juice
1 slice of pink grapefruit, for garnish

Glassware: Collins glass

Fill the glass with ice then add the vodka or gin. Pour in the grapefruit juice then stir using a barspoon. Garnish with a slice of pink grapefruit.

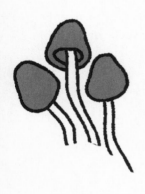

THE CRUEL QUINCE DAIQUIRI

THE CRUEL PRINCE BY HOLLY BLACK

In a concoction befitting Holly Black's high cheek-boned antagonist, razor-sharp quince and lime give way to the irresistible charm of sugar and rum. Take this as fair warning: no good comes to the girl who tastes this deceptively delicate cocktail.

1¾ ounces white rum
3½ teaspoons quince preserves
⅔ ounce lime juice
½ ounce simple syrup
1 lime wedge, for garnish

Glassware: Martini glass or Champagne coupe

Add all the ingredients to a cocktail shaker filled with ice. Shake hard until well mixed (you may need to stir afterward to ensure the preserves are fully dissolved into the other ingredients). Double-strain into a chilled martini glass or Champagne coupe. Classically the Daiquiri is garnished with a lime wedge on the rim of the glass, but perhaps faerie fruit might better suit your purposes . . .

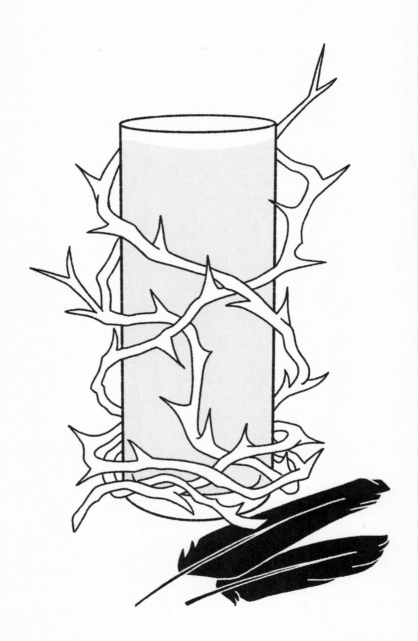

THE WICKED SLING

THE WICKED KING BY HOLLY BLACK

Back for more, are we? Unsurprising really. Despite your complicated feelings, you're as bound to this boozy cocktail as you are to the new—and equally boozy—High King. So better drink this series in, you'll never get sick of it.

1 ounce gin
¼ ounce Cointreau
¼ ounce Benedictine
½ ounce Heering cherry liqueur
½ ounce lime juice
⅓ ounce grenadine
1 dash Angostura bitters
4 ounces pineapple juice
1 orange or lemon slice, for garnish
1 maraschino cherry, for garnish

Glassware: Highball or sling glass

Add all the ingredients to a cocktail shaker. Add ice, shake, and strain into a highball or sling glass filled with ice. Serve with a fruit slice (orange or lemon) and the maraschino cherry.

Vampiro

The Serpent and the Wings of Night
by Carissa Broadbent

Heroine Oraya knows all too well the dangers—and delights—of a bloodthirsty lover. With sweet, savory, and spice forming an unholy alliance in this succulent tipple, you just might find out too.

2 ounces tequila reposado
1 ounce tomato juice
1 ounce orange juice
½ ounce lime juice
½ ounce grenadine syrup
7 dashes hot pepper sauce
Pinch of salt
Grind of black pepper
1 lime wedge, for garnish

Glassware: Old-Fashioned glass

Fill a cocktail shaker with ice. Add all the ingredients and shake until cold. Strain into an Old-Fashioned glass filled with ice and add the lime wedge as garnish.

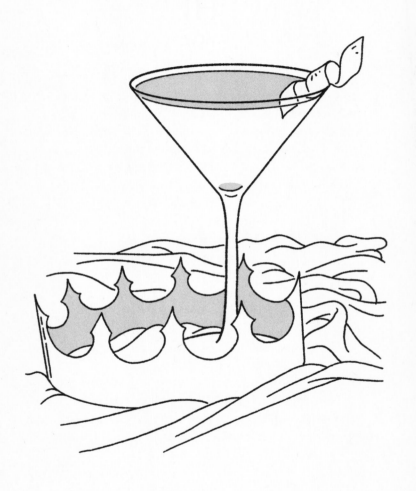

BEAST BETWEEN the SHEETS

LEDGE BY STACEY MCEWAN

This cocktail is a little unusual in that it mixes two different species—sorry—spirits! It therefore has some serious teeth to it (or should we say talons), yet when made properly, it is a well-balanced and smooth libation. And if Ryon is anything to go by, being unusual only makes you more swoon-worthy.

⅔ ounce white rum
⅔ ounce Cognac
⅔ ounce Cointreau
⅓ ounce lemon juice
1 lemon twist, for garnish

Glassware: Martini glass or Champagne coupe

Add all the ingredients to a cocktail shaker. Add ice and shake well. Double-strain into your glass, which must be chilled to a glacial temperature. Garnish with the lemon twist.

MAI TAI-RANT

GILD BY RAVEN KENNEDY

Like King Midas himself, it'd be easy to mistake the Mai Tai for an easygoing, light, and fruity cocktail, a fitting beverage for a guest of his majesty. But in reality, it's a strong, rum-based, tiki-style drink most suited to dark or golden rum, with bold-as-brass flavor. The garnish of the half lime carcass serves as fair warning: its superficial sweetness will be used against you.

1 ounce Jamaican gold rum
1 ounce agricole rum
1 ounce lime juice, juiced lime reserved for garnish
½ ounce curaçao
⅓ ounce orgeat syrup
⅓ ounce simple syrup
1 mint sprig, for garnish

Glassware: Rocks glass

Add all the ingredients to a cocktail shaker. Reserve half of a lime for garnish. Add crushed or cracked ice and shake well. Strain into a rocks glass filled with ice and garnish with half of the "spent" lime and the mint sprig.

FINE, MAKE ME YOUR VESPER

SHADOW AND BONE BY LEIGH BARDUGO

Best served as cold as you can possibly get it, this is a classic cocktail just as powerful as *Shadow and Bone*'s insatiable villain, the Darkling. Don't forget the lemon twist over the top to add some much-needed citrus sunshine.

2 ounces gin
⅔ ounce vodka
⅓ ounce Lillet Blanc
1 lemon twist, for garnish

Glassware: Martini glass, goblet, or wine glass

Shake all the ingredients with ice in a shaker, and double-strain into a chilled martini glass, goblet, or wine glass. Add the lemon twist over the top to provide the drink with lift from the citrus oils.

GREEN-EYED FAERIE
A COURT OF THORNS AND ROSES
BY SARAH J. MAAS

Oh Tamlin. What lies behind that glittering mask of gold and emerald, behind those piercing green eyes? Impossible beast or handsome young warrior, serve this iconic tipple and you might just find out.

1 ounce absinthe
1 ounce chilled water
1 ounce lemon juice
⅔ ounce simple syrup
1 dash Angostura bitters
½ egg white
1 lemon twist or gold edible glitter, for garnish

Glassware: Martini glass or Champagne coupe

Add all the ingredients to a cocktail shaker. Shake without ice (dry shake), then add ice and shake again (wet shake). Strain into a chilled martini glass or Champagne coupe. Garnish with the lemon twist or a sprinkling of gold edible glitter as a delicious homage to the High Lord who started it all.

THE DEVIL
WITHIN ME
ONE DARK WINDOW BY RACHEL GILLIG

Diligent readers will now be well versed in what to serve
any seductive villain who darkens your door. But what
tipple do you turn to when the monster might actually be
you? Known in Mexico as "El Diablo," this thirst-
quencher cocktail certainly won't clear your head, but it
may help weaken the malevolent spirit living rent-free in
your mind. Handily it's also very easy to make, so if you
hear any psychic protests along the lines of "But I protect
you," just grab the crème de cassis, girl, he's lying.

2 ounces tequila
1 ounce crème de cassis
1 ounce lime juice
Ginger ale, to top
1 lime wedge, for garnish

Glassware: Highball glass

Add the tequila, crème de cassis, and lime juice to a
highball glass filled with ice. Top with ginger ale and
garnish with the lime wedge.

A
TOAST
to
BITTER
RIVALS

SHE'S GOT a CONCEALED WEAPON

THRONE OF GLASS BY SARAH J. MAAS

This high-octane cocktail may appear, at first glance, to be nothing more than a regular girly pink martini, but it's simply playing a part. The concealed weapon here—rather than a career as an assassin carefully hidden from the king's court—is a single shot of absinthe. Underestimate it at your peril.

1 ounce absinthe
1 ounce Chambord liqueur
⅔ ounce lemon juice
½ ounce simple syrup
1 dash Angostura bitters
1 dash Peychaud's bitters
½ egg white
1 lemon twist, for garnish

Glassware: Martini glass or Champagne coupe

Add all the ingredients to a cocktail shaker. Shake without ice (dry shake), then add ice and shake again (wet shake). Strain into a chilled martini glass or Champagne coupe. Garnish with the lemon twist.

Viscous Little Thing

POWERLESS BY LAUREN ROBERTS

Much like Paedyn Gray and Kai Azer, you'll be powerless to resist the obvious chemistry between sharp lime, fiery tequila, and the wonderfully smooth, creamy texture of emulsified egg white in this tequila sour. A knife to the throat need not be used to gulp this one down.

2 ounces tequila
1 ounce lime juice
⅔ ounce simple syrup
1 egg white

Glassware: Rocks glass

Add all the ingredients to a cocktail shaker. Shake without ice (dry shake), then add ice and shake again (wet shake). Strain into a rocks glass over ice.

ONCE UPON a BRAMBLE HEART

ONCE UPON A BROKEN HEART
BY STEPHANIE GARBER

This drink is incredibly easy to make, just like the deal
Evangeline strikes with the Prince of Hearts to stop her
true love marrying another. But unlike cocktails, fairy
tales aren't so straightforward, especially when
a trickster immortal wishes to use you in his
dangerous games . . .

2 ounces gin
1 ounce lemon juice
½ ounce simple syrup
½ ounce crème de mûre or crème de cassis liqueur
1 lemon wedge, for garnish
1 fresh raspberry, for garnish

Glassware: Rocks glass

Shake the gin, lemon juice, and simple syrup together in
a cocktail shaker filled with ice. Strain into a rocks glass
filled with ice. Stir. Add more crushed ice so that the glass is
full. Trickle the crème de mûre over the top and garnish with
the lemon wedge and raspberry, to symbolize all of our
wounded hearts.

THE BALLAD of NEGRONI AFTER

THE BALLAD OF NEVER AFTER
BY STEPHANIE GARBER

Having to team up once again with the very person who stole your chance at happily ever after is a bitter pill to swallow. Luckily, this is the perfect, and equally bitter, drink to round off a day of battling a curse, an untrustworthy partner, and your own desires.

1 ounce gin
1 ounce Campari
1 ounce sweet vermouth
1 orange wedge or twist, for garnish

Glassware: Rocks glass

Add all of the ingredients to an ice-filled rocks glass and stir (one or two large ice cubes are much better than a lot of small ones here). Garnish with the orange wedge or twist.

GIRL, GODDESS, GIBSON

GIRL, GODDESS, QUEEN BY BEA FITZGERALD

To hell with love and predictably sweet cocktails! If
Persephone can jump headfirst into the Underworld and
strong-arm its rude yet frustratingly sexy ruler Hades,
you can enjoy this classic martini with a surprisingly
tangy twist.

⅓ ounce dry vermouth
2 ounces gin
Pickled cocktail onion, for garnish

Glassware: Martini glass

Fill a mixing glass with ice, add the vermouth and stir to
coat the ice. If at this point you want to make a drier
martini, you would strain out some of the vermouth and discard it. Add the gin and stir until chilled and diluted—you
want to take some of the "edge" off the neat gin. Strain into
a chilled martini glass and defiantly garnish with the onion.

GRUMPY WANTS TEQUILA SUNSHINE

EMILY WILDE'S ENCYCLOPAEDIA OF FAERIES
BY HEATHER FAWCETT

This cocktail is as easy to drink as it is easy to make, and while it's not the most sophisticated beverage in the world, it's fun. And sometimes that's exactly what you need. Come on, put away the field journal, suppress the eye roll, and observe the charming magic of grenadine and orange juice creating a color gradient in your glass. We know you want to.

1¾ ounces tequila
2½ ounces orange juice
1 barspoon of grenadine

Glassware: Highball glass

Add the tequila and orange juice to a cocktail shaker. Fill with ice and shake. Strain into a highball glass filled with ice. Pour the grenadine into the top of the glass; it is a dense, sticky syrup and will therefore sink to the bottom, creating the desired sunshine effect.

BRANDY BANTER
THE SONG OF THE MARKED BY S. M. GAITHER

The Brandy Banter is unique as it is one of very few cocktails where you attend to the elaborate garnish first before the drink itself. So if you're someone who likes their romance precluded by plenty of quick quips and snarky delights, we thoroughly recommend pairing Cas and Elander's adorable dynamic with this sharp sugar-crusted concoction.

1 lemon, for garnish
Sugar, for garnish
1¾ ounces Cognac
⅔ ounce lemon juice
2 or 3 dashes triple sec
2 or 3 dashes maraschino liqueur
1 or 2 dashes simple syrup
2 dashes Boker's bitters

Glassware: Martini glass or Champagne coupe

Prepare your garnish: find a lemon that fits snugly into the top of the glass you intend to use, and cut a thick wheel from the middle. Hollow out the middle, removing all of the flesh and the majority of the pith. Juice the flesh onto a small plate (this will adhere the sugar to the lemon shell and glass rim). Place into the glass with a sliver of peel above the rim (this is why it's important that the lemon peel fits well into the glass). Dip the top of the peel and the glass into the lemon juice, then into the sugar to create a sugar rim. If you leave this for a couple of hours, you'll be left with a pretty hard crust of sugar around the rim, which has the advantage of not sweetening your drink too much when you're ready to drink it; however, it also makes it a little more difficult to clean!

Add all the ingredients to a cocktail shaker filled with ice. Shake hard and double-strain into the prepared glass.

THE GAUNTLET GIMLET

FOURTH WING BY REBECCA YARROS

Officers in the navy adopted the Gimlet as their own for its vitamin C and ability to be preserved during long voyages. Similarly, the Gauntlet Gimlet is a wonderful fortifier for the elite of Navarre's army: dragon riders. A powerful nip of Dutch courage for any unlikely squad member, it might just help you survive the brutal challenges at Basgiath War College and your fellow murderous cadets.

2 ounces navy-strength gin
2 ounces Rose's lime juice cordial

Glassware: Martini glass or Champagne coupe

Add the gin and lime juice cordial ingredients to a mixing glass filled with ice and stir until well chilled. Strain into your chilled glass.

THE APEROL SIX
THE ATLAS SIX BY OLIVIE BLAKE

A guaranteed crowd-pleaser, this is a fitting cocktail to
serve your very hot magical secret society. The below
recipe makes a decent-sized glass, but if you want to make
a jug to share with the rest of your dangerous fellowship,
just remember the ratio of 3:2:1 (prosecco:spirit:soda).
So pop the prosecco and get pouring—oh dear, are there
only five glasses?

3 ounces prosecco
2 ounces Aperol
1 ounce soda water
1 orange wedge or slice, for garnish

Glassware: Cocktail glass of your choice

Add all the ingredients to a cocktail glass filled with
ice. Stir and garnish with the orange wedge or slice.

MAGICAL MANHATTAN

One for My Enemy by Olivie Blake

A chance encounter with this cocktail could reignite a devastating magical conflict the likes of which the criminal underbelly of Manhattan has never seen before. Families will be torn apart and sacrifices will be made. But it will be worth it, because revenge mixed with this much love has never tasted so sweet.

2 ounces bourbon or rye
⅔ ounce sweet vermouth
2 or 3 dashes Angostura bitters
1 maraschino cherry, for garnish

Glassware: Cocktail glass of your choice

Fill a mixing glass with ice. Add all of the ingredients and stir until chilled. Strain into a chilled cocktail glass and garnish with the maraschino cherry for an extra dash of sweetness and forbidden romance.

FRUITS
of the
FAE

BLOODY FAERIE

FAEBOUND BY SAARA EL-ARIFI

An elven warrior may be forgiven for dismissing this classic cocktail as nothing but a strangely savory relic of the past. Yet the luxurious mouthfeel of tomato juice with the spice of Tabasco and tang of lemon is just perfect for a lazy late brunch or a morning pick-me-up after an exile. The truth is this cocktail has endured for a reason; it's a truly seductive combination of heartening and intoxicating.

1¾ ounces vodka
3½ ounces tomato juice
4 to 10 dashes Tabasco (depending on
how hot you want things to get)
2 to 5 dashes Worcestershire sauce
A splash of lemon juice
1 or 2 grinds of black pepper
A pinch of salt (celery salt works well if you have it)
1 celery stick, for garnish

Glassware: Highball glass

Add all the ingredients to a cocktail shaker, but go slowly with the Tabasco and Worcestershire sauces, so you get the spice just how you like it. You might want to play around with the quantity of lemon juice too. Add ice and roll the cocktail shaker, turning it over slowly to allow the ingredients to mix and chill—don't go nuts and shake it as you'll make the drink too watery. Strain into a chilled highball glass, with or without ice. A celery stick is the classic garnish, but you can be more inventive and use whatever you have captive in your fridge.

'SMASH ME

SHATTER ME BY TAHEREH MAFI

This bourbon cocktail requires a gentle, yet ultimately lethal touch. Mint and raspberries are muddled together to form a taste so beautifully bright and refreshing, even the loneliest of girls would forget their confines after taking a sip. Raspberries are preferred but feel free to use any berry you can (safely) get your hands on.

5 or 6 berries (raspberries preferred)
6 to 8 mint leaves
2 ounces bourbon
1 ounce lime juice
¾ ounce simple syrup
1 lime wedge and/or mint sprig, for garnish

Glassware: Highball glass

Gently muddle the raspberries and mint in the bottom of a cocktail shaker. Be careful not to overly muddle the mint, as it will bring out bitter flavors from the leaves. Add the bourbon, lime juice, and simple syrup, along with ice. Shake and strain into an ice-filled highball glass. Garnish with the lime wedge or mint sprig (or both!). If you use a mint sprig, agitate the leaves by slapping the sprig against your hand to release the mint oils and aromas, then place it next to the straw.

THE PRIORY of the ORANGE-TINI

THE PRIORY OF THE ORANGE TREE
BY SAMANTHA SHANNON

Whether you're a dragon rider, a secret guard to the Queen, or tasked with furthering a thousand-year-old bloodline to protect the realm, this is the ideal cocktail for a woman trying to keep up with life's demands. Marmalade makes this playful martini dangerously drinkable and puts the possibility of love amidst so many spinning plates at an all-time high.

1¾ ounces gin
½ ounce Cointreau
½ ounce lemon juice
1 barspoon or teaspoon orange marmalade
1 strip of orange zest, for garnish

Glassware: Martini glass or Champagne coupe

Add all the ingredients to a cocktail shaker filled with ice. Shake hard and double-strain into a chilled martini glass or Champagne coupe. Garnish with the strip of orange zest.

HIGH LADY

A COURT OF MIST AND FURY BY SARAH J. MAAS

Wedding preparations are well underway and the
question of a possible High Lady is on everyone's lips.
After all, what would be better to toast to High Fae
nuptials with than this classically elegant cocktail?

1¾ ounces gin
⅔ ounce lemon juice
⅔ ounce triple sec
1 egg white (optional)
1 strip of lemon zest, for garnish

Glassware: Martini glass or Champagne coupe

Add all the ingredients to a cocktail shaker. Shake
without ice (dry shake), then add ice and shake again
(wet shake). Strain into a chilled martini glass or Champagne coupe. Garnish with the strip of lemon zest.

CRESCENT CITY COSMOPOLITAN

HOUSE OF EARTH AND BLOOD
BY SARAH J. MAAS

Do as the Lunathions do and savor every pleasure
Crescent City has to offer with this light and cooling
Cosmo. Things might get dark, your drink's crimson
contents may be spilt (it is the House of Earth and Blood
after all) but you can always count on a gorgeous fallen
angel to help you fight your demons.

1 ounce vodka
½ ounce triple sec
½ ounce lime juice
1 ounce cranberry juice
1 orange twist, for garnish

Glassware: Martini glass

Put all the ingredients into a cocktail shaker filled
with ice. Shake well and strain into a chilled martini
glass. Garnish with the orange twist.

FLAME HOUSE PUNCH

HOUSE OF FLAME AND SHADOW
BY SARAH J. MAAS

If you're ready to really light it up, we highly recommend
the Flame House Punch. This rum-based cocktail is so
strong it might just send you to another galaxy. If that
seems a little unsafe however, follow Bryce's lead and grip
onto the juicy flavor of peach for some stability.

1 ounce lemon juice
1 ounce dark rum
⅔ ounce Cognac
⅓ ounce peach brandy or crème de pêche
⅓ ounce simple syrup
1 ounce water

Glassware: Highball glass

Add all the ingredients to a cocktail shaker. Add ice
and shake (be careful to dodge the lightning), then
strain into a highball glass filled with ice.

You Hit Me Like a Hurricane

The Hurricane Wars by Thea Guanzon

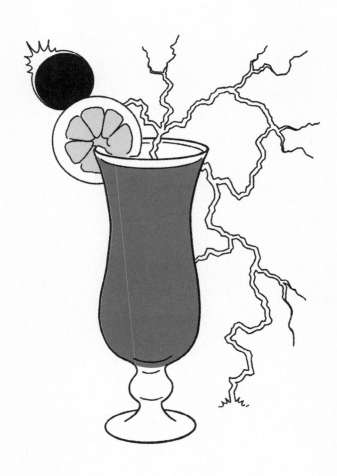

In this cocktail, warring forces of light and dark rum combine to create something so intoxicating it may just take down an empire. You may be forgiven for thinking this is just a storm in a tea cup, but trust us, when you first see the magic of dark, sticky grenadine sliding down sunshine yellow fruit juices, the tension will be almost too much to bear. Just ask Talasyn and Alaric.

1¾ ounces dark rum
1¾ ounces light rum
1¾ ounces passion fruit juice
1 ounce orange juice
½ ounce lime juice
1 barspoon grenadine
1 orange slice, for garnish
1 maraschino cherry, for garnish

Glassware: Hurricane or highball glass

Add all the ingredients except for the grenadine to a cocktail shaker. Add ice, shake, and strain into a hurricane or highball glass filled with ice. Pour the grenadine into the top of the glass (it is a dense, sticky syrup and will therefore sink to the bottom with glee). Serve with the orange slice and maraschino cherry.

PINE AFTER COLADA

THIS WOVEN KINGDOM BY TAHEREH MAFI

Prince Kamran can't get the beguiling servant girl with the strange eyes out of his head. Who, or what, is she? And what does she have to do with a deadly prophecy that threatens the kingdom? Kamran should know that amidst the infatuation, the burning desire that feels like madness, you've got to have a little lighthearted fun! Luckily, the Pine After Colada provides a wonderfully sweet relief from even the deepest of yearnings.

1¾ ounces white rum
1¾ ounces heavy cream
5 ounces pineapple juice
1 paper umbrella, for garnish (optional)
Pineapple slices, for garnish (optional)

Glassware: Highball or hurricane glass

Add all the ingredients to a cocktail shaker. Add ice and shake well. Strain into a highball or hurricane glass filled with ice. Remember, you've got to have fun with this cocktail, so go wild with garnishes; paper umbrellas, pineapple slices, or perhaps a bejeweled garland of the finest silks might feel more appropriate?

NINTH COCKTAIL
NINTH HOUSE BY LEIGH BARDUGO

This is not the kind of beer cocktail that appears in your average student union bar. Greengages are a type of plum that are sweet and rich; their flavor especially appeals to the kind of privileged palates that might haunt the halls of Yale. The greengage liqueur used in this recipe is made by Bramley & Gage. If you can't get hold of any and wish to survive on campus, then substitute it with a couple of teaspoons of greengage jam—or plum jam if you can bear it.

1 ounce bourbon
1 ounce greengage liqueur
½ ounce lemon juice
⅓ ounce agave syrup
2 ounces ginger ale, to top
Lager, to top

Glassware: Highball or half-pint glass

Add the bourbon, greengage liqueur, lemon juice, and agave syrup to a cocktail shaker. Add ice and shake well. Strain into a highball or half-pint glass filled with ice. Top with the ginger ale and lager.

CURSED FOREST MOJITO

WHERE THE DARK STANDS STILL

BY A. B. PORANEK

If you go down to the woods today, you'll find a mojito
in disguise. Swapping traditional soda for cherry cola,
and the sugar for black currant jam, this sumptuous
tipple is so rich in fruity flavor you'll barely notice being
whisked away by the demon warden of the wood. But
once you're inside his dark crumbling mansion, well,
that's another matter.

2 ounces rum
1 ounce lemon juice
8 mint leaves
Spoonful of black currant or blackberry jam
Cherry cola, to top

Glassware: Highball glass

Add the rum, lemon juice, mint leaves, and black currant jam to a highball glass. Add crushed ice and
churn with a barspoon. Top with cherry cola.

SCRUMPT

OUS

SPRITZES

A COUPE of THORNS and ROSÉ

A COURT OF THORNS AND ROSES

BY SARAH J. MAAS

It's the summer solstice party; you're looking positively fae and its time to let your hair down. There really is no better beverage for the occasion than a crisp, sparkling glass of faerie wine. Known for its euphoric properties, this cocktail will get you dancing for your High Lord in no time at all.

1½ ounces silver tequila
⅔ ounce cranberry juice
½ ounce lemon juice
⅓ ounce simple syrup
2 ounces brut rosé sparkling wine, to top

Glassware: Champagne coupe

Add the tequila, cranberry juice, lemon juice, and simple syrup into a shaker filled with ice and shake until well-chilled. Strain into a Champagne coupe. Top with the sparkling rosé.

Mortal Mule

CITY OF BONES BY CASSANDRA CLARE

Like *The Mortal Instruments* series, this simple yet
wonderfully layered cocktail has swept the globe.
With a spicy kick from the ginger, a citrus zest from the
lime, and a clean booze hit from the vodka, the Mortal
Mule is just as dangerous and irresistible as the most
proficient of demon hunters. A helpful reminder:
if you're making this cocktail in the hopes of going
to bone city and would like that special someone to
rip their clothes off, all you need to do is ask.

1¾ ounces vodka
½ lime, juiced
Ginger beer, to top
1 slice of lime, for garnish
1 dash Angostura bitters (optional)
1 mint sprig, for garnish

Glassware: Highball glass or small punch cup

Add the vodka and lime juice to your glass. Fill with
ice and top with ginger beer. You can add Angostura
bitters, if you like an extra herby kick. Add the slice of lime
and mint sprig, to garnish.

MOURNING GLORY FIZZ

BELLADONNA BY ADALYN GRACE

Death is inevitable, but as Signa Farrow is here to show us, he's also pretty hot. So instead of moping alone over another guardian's untimely end, why not mix up this cocktail and enjoy a good old-fashioned murder investigation with the gorgeous Grim Reaper himself?

2 ounces Scotch
½ ounce lemon juice
½ ounce lime juice
½ ounce simple syrup
1 egg white
1 or 2 dashes absinthe
Soda water, to top

Glassware: Highball glass

Add all the ingredients except the soda water to a cocktail shaker. Shake without ice to emulsify the egg white. Add ice and shake again. Strain into a highball glass (no ice), and top with soda water.

SHAPE-SHIFTER SPRITZ

ZODIAC ACADEMY: THE AWAKENING
BY CAROLINE PECKHAM AND
SUSANNE VALENTI

It can be hard to not break a sweat when an achingly hot dragon shifter has you in his crosshairs. Enter the Shape-Shifter Spritz, the only antidote to airs of entitlement, intense gazes, and stacked muscles. So let him use you as target practice, this tall drink of elderflower-laced soda water will keep as cool as its cucumber garnish.

1¼ ounces Suze
½ ounce elderflower cordial
1¾ ounces English sparkling wine
1¾ ounces soda water
A wedge of grapefruit
1 cucumber slice, for garnish

Glassware: Collins glass

Pour all the ingredients over cubed ice in a glass. Stir well. Squeeze a wedge of grapefruit into the cocktail and garnish with the cucumber slice.

THE KIR of NOTHING

THE QUEEN OF NOTHING BY HOLLY BLACK

Breakups are tough, especially if, like Holly Black's
heroine Jude, your wicked faerie king has broken your
crown as well as your heart. But even queens of nothing
deserve a treat. So stop bingeing reality television, pop
the Champagne, and pour yourself a drink that's as regal
as you are. It's time to grab that bridle and show him
who's really in charge.

½ ounce crème de cassis
Champagne, to top
1 fresh raspberry, for garnish

Glassware: Champagne flute

Pour the crème de cassis into the Champagne flute
and top with Champagne. Crown with the raspberry.

AMBROSIA
NEON GODS BY KATEE ROBERT

One of the lesser-known classics, the Ambrosia is a
glittering Champagne cocktail named after the drink of
the gods. According to Greek mythology, any mortal who
drank ambrosia became immortal. And after reading
what Hades does to Persephone in Katee Robert's red-hot
retelling, you'll be on your knees, begging for a sip. We've
heard one taste is all you need . . .

1 ounce Cognac
1 ounce Calvados
2 or 3 dashes triple sec
2 or 3 dashes lemon juice
Champagne, to top

Glassware: Champagne flute or coupe

Pour the Cognac, Calvados, triple sec, and lemon
juice into a cocktail shaker. Add ice and shake well.
Strain into a chilled Champagne flute or coupe and top with
Champagne.

SCARLET COLLINS

THESE VIOLENT DELIGHTS BY CHLOE GONG

The versatility of a Tom Collins lies in the fact that you can not only mix things up by changing the base spirit (vodka, bourbon, whiskey, and tequila all work well), but you can also use different sweetening agents. The below version is a fitting tribute to Chloe Gong's Scarlet Gang; it's a cruel crimson beauty that hides the deadly strength of pink gin behind the sweetness of pomegranate and cherry liqueur. We can't think of a more opulent Collins to swear your allegiance to.

2 ounces pink gin
2 ounces pomegranate juice
1 ounce lemon juice
¾ ounce maraschino liqueur
Soda water, to top
1 maraschino cherry, for garnish

Glassware: Highball glass

Fill a highball glass two-thirds full with ice. Add the gin, pomegranate juice, lemon juice, and maraschino liqueur. Top with soda, add more ice if necessary to fill the glass, and stir to mix. Garnish with the maraschino cherry or, if you've twisted it up using a different liqueur, anything appropriate. Just don't expect your disloyalty to go unpunished.

HUNT ME on DARK and STORMY WATERS

HUNT ON DARK WATERS BY KATEE ROBERT

Very difficult to mess up, a Dark and Stormy is the ideal cocktail for anyone who's made one too many mistakes recently, such as stealing from your vampire ex or falling into another realm. It's also a brilliant drink to share with new friends, like the dark band of paladin pirates that have just fished you out of the sea. Make sure to pour an extra-large glass for their telekinetic captain; he looks like he knows his way around a portal.

5 ounces ginger beer
½ ounce lime juice
1¾ ounces dark rum

Glassware: Highball glass

Fill a highball glass with ice. Pour in the ginger beer, leaving space for the lime juice and rum. Squeeze in the lime juice then slowly pour over the dark rum to float it on top.

A MARVELLOUS, LIGHT LEMONADE
A MARVELLOUS LIGHT BY FREYA MARSKE

This might not be the most elegant of drinks (those with a more Edwardian sensibility might argue that lemonade is not for grown-ups) and it might seem, well, a bit sour. But, just like Edwin Courcey, it has magical hidden depths. The perfect light and refreshing drink, it deserves to be given a chance.

1½ ounces Jack Daniel's whiskey
¾ ounce triple sec
1 ounce lemon juice
Lemonade, to top
1 lemon wheel or wedge, for garnish

Glassware: Highball glass

Add the whiskey, triple sec, and lemon juice to a cocktail shaker. Add ice and shake well. Strain into a highball glass filled with ice and top with lemonade. Stir gently and garnish with the lemon wheel or wedge.

A TWINKLE of FROST and STARLIGHT

A COURT OF FROST AND STARLIGHT
BY SARAH J. MAAS

Just like Sarah J. Maas's refreshing companion tale, the sweet and sparkling Twinkle is not to be missed. The incorporation of vodka and Champagne with the liqueur of snow-white elderflower creates the perfect cocktail for the Winter Solstice and the opening of presents (or in Rhysand's case, the undressing of presents).

1 ounce vodka
½ ounce elderflower liqueur or cordial
Champagne (about 2½ ounces), to top
1 long lemon twist, for garnish

Glassware: Champagne flute or coupe

Add the vodka and elderflower liqueur to a cocktail shaker filled with ice. Shake well and double-strain into a chilled Champagne flute or coupe. Top with Champagne. Garnish with the lemon twist.

TOE-CURLING TIPPLES

HAIR of the WOLF
BONDED BY THORNS BY ELIZABETH HELEN

After spending each night as a pack of demonic wolves, it's really no surprise your four fae princes are feeling the worse for wear. To break the curse and get the reverse harem underway (because really, why should you choose?), prescribe them this spicy nineteenth-century hangover cure.

½ ounce Cognac
2 or 3 dashes vinegar (any kind)
4 or 5 dashes Worcestershire sauce
3 to 5 dashes Tabasco
Pinch of salt
Pinch of freshly ground black pepper
1 egg yolk

Glassware: Small glass of your choice

Add the Cognac, vinegar, Worcestershire sauce, Tabasco, salt, and pepper to a small glass. Stir to combine, then crack the egg and separate the yolk before dropping it into the mixture raw and gobbling down the whole thing.

LITTLE SCORPION
THE FAMILIAR BY LEIGH BARDUGO

A cocktail with old-world glamour, the Scorpion was typically served as a punch for several people, garnished with gardenia flowers. The recipe below makes a standalone serving—a Little Scorpion, if you will. But don't worry; it has just as much of a seductive sting, and like Santángel, you won't have the sense to stay away.

1¾ ounces white rum
⅔ ounce brandy or Cognac
1¾ ounces orange juice
1 ounce lemon juice
⅔ ounce orgeat syrup
1 edible flower, for garnish

Glassware: Highball glass

Add all the ingredients to a cocktail shaker. Add ice and shake well before straining into an ice-filled highball glass. Garnish with the edible flower for a touch of romance.

'NOGKILLER
GODKILLER BY HANNAH KANER

Like Kissen, eggnog is a quirky character with history,
the cocktail's association with Christmas going all the
way back to the 1700s. It's also not the simplest of drinks
to get on with, so it works better in a group setting as the
effort (or angst) per drink is vastly reduced. Perhaps an
equally tortured warrior-turned-baker could provide a
few mince pies to help this festive love-in along?

½ ounce cup sugar
12 eggs
12 ounces Cognac
4 ounces dark rum
2 cups heavy cream
2 cups whole milk
Freshly grated nutmeg, for garnish

Glassware: Small glasses or punch cups

In a large mixing bowl or punch bowl, whisk the sugar
into the eggs and beat in the alcohol. Add the cream and
beat again. Add the milk and beat a final time. Ladle into
ice-filled glasses. Garnish each glass with freshly grated
nutmeg just before serving.

ƐMPYREAN ƐSPRESSO MARTINI

IRON FLAME BY REBECCA YARROS

Once in a while there's a cocktail so perfect it's impossible not to imbue it with the unapproachable splendor of heaven itself. No human knows the exact machinations of this fiery meeting of caffeine and vodka, but what we do know is this drink will get you through graduation and possibly a revolution.

2 ounces vodka
1 ounce espresso
1 ounce coffee liqueur
½ ounce simple syrup
4 coffee beans, for garnish

Glassware: Martini glass

Fill a cocktail shaker with ice. Add all the ingredients and shake until cold. Strain into a chilled martini glass and add the coffee beans on top.

ALE of TWIN CITIES
IMMORTAL LONGINGS BY CHLOE GONG

Lime, apple, malted barley, bitters, and nettle—they might have competing agendas but when flavors are this jam-packed, you know sparks are going to fly! Trust us, the extra steps are worth it (as they say, San-Er wasn't built in a day). Just think carefully about whose body you're jumping into, or onto, afterward . . .

⅔ ounce lime juice
½ ounce homemade nettle cordial (see opposite)
2½ ounces apple cider
½ ounce malted barley syrup
2½ ounces vodka
1 ounce Punt e Mes sweet vermouth
2 dashes Angostura bitters

Glassware: Half-pint tankard or glass

Chill a half-pint tankard or beer mug. Add the lime juice, nettle cordial, apple juice, and malted barley syrup to a cocktail shaker. Stir to dissolve the thick malt syrup, then add the vodka, vermouth, bitters, and plenty of ice, and shake hard. Strain into the chilled tankard.

NETTLE CORDIAL

2½ cups fresh nettle leaves
1¼ cups granulated sugar
3¼ teaspoons citric acid
7 ounces water

Wash the nettles, removing any damaged leaves or thick stems, and roughly chop them. Add the sugar, citric acid, and water to a saucepan and heat until boiling. Let cool to about 160°F. Add the chopped nettles and stir. Once cool, add the mixture to an airtight jar. Leave in a cool, dark place for 1 to 2 days, agitating or shaking it now and again. Strain through a sieve or piece of muslin if you have it. Add 1 ounce of vodka to help preserve the cordial (but only if you're using it for boozy cocktails!) and it will last for 3 to 4 weeks in the fridge.

RANDY ALEXANDRIAN

THE ATLAS PARADOX BY OLIVIE BLAKE

The Randy Alexandrian is rich and creamy, with subtle chocolate notes. It's a treat usually best enjoyed later in the evening, when the hours—or decades, even—blend together and texts from exes hold extra potency. But if Olivie Blake's utterly moreish sequel has taught us anything, it's that traveling back in time only leads to heartbreak, so swerve the ex and pour yourself another drink instead!

1½ ounces brandy
1 ounce crème de cacao white
1 ounce heavy cream
Freshly grated nutmeg, for garnish

Glassware: Champagne coupe

Fill a cocktail shaker with ice, add all the ingredients, and shake until cold. Strain into a Champagne coupe and dust with freshly grated nutmeg.

ONE HELL of a SOUR

HELL BENT BY LEIGH BARDUGO

Sure, it's easy to be cynical. Maybe you want to write off this cocktail as a rich, self-regarding drink that thinks a little too much of itself (why is there egg AND Merlot?!), but once it disappears, you might just find yourself missing what you had. Maybe this devilishly red sour, like Darlington, is well worth going to hell and back for.

2 ounces whiskey, bourbon, or rye
1 ounce lemon juice
⅔ ounce simple syrup
1 egg white
½ ounce red wine (fruity reds like Merlot
or Malbec work well)

Glassware: Rocks glass

Add the whiskey, lemon juice, simple syrup, and egg white to a cocktail shaker. Shake without ice (dry shake), then add ice and shake again (wet shake). Strain into a rocks glass over ice and gently add the red wine over a barspoon to float.

SAINTS au CHAMPAGNE

THE CURSE OF SAINTS BY KATE DRAMIS

A slightly naughty and deliciously divine twist on the Soyer au Champagne, this is a late-night dessert cocktail for you to selflessly make your friends, rivals, or love triangle. Blending with the Champagne aerates the ice cream and makes it so cool and fluffy it may compel a lover to burn the world down for you, but alas, that is the curse of saints.

8 ounces cider brandy (Calvados or Cognac will also work)
4 scoops of vanilla ice cream
2 ounces curaçao (or use triple sec)
2 ounces simple syrup
10 ounces Champagne
1 dash of Angostura bitters

Glassware: Champagne coupes

Add the cider brandy, ice cream, curaçao, simple syrup, and Champagne to a blender and blend on high speed for 10 to 20 seconds. Pour into Champagne coupes and add a dash of bitters to each drink.

A VIOLENT END in the AFTERNOON

OUR VIOLENT ENDS BY CHLOE GONG

As Juliette and Roma have taught us, there's a fine line between love and hate, between wanting someone dead and wanting to kiss them. Luckily this absinthe-based cocktail really can take the edge off a violent passion, just as the inclusion of citrus handily takes the edge off the absinthe. Just as well when you've got more monsters to battle.

½ ounce absinthe
⅔ ounce lemon juice
⅓ ounce simple syrup
Champagne, to top

Glassware: Champagne flute

Add the absinthe, lemon juice, and simple syrup to a cocktail shaker. Add ice and shake well. Strain into a chilled Champagne flute and top with Champagne.

WHITE LIES
GODKILLER BY HANNAH KANER

What? you might be thinking. *Coffee, vodka, and CREAM?* You hate creamy drinks, always have. But sometimes you just can't predict who or what's going to join your quest. It might be what is essentially a vodka milkshake; it might be an oddly adorable god of white lies. Don't kill either before you give them a chance, and make sure to freshly grate your nutmeg. It makes the cocktail (sorry, Skedi) irresistible.

1½ ounces vodka
¾ ounce coffee liqueur
¾ ounce half-and-half
Freshly grated nutmeg, for garnish

Glassware: Rocks glass

Add the vodka and coffee liqueur to a rocks glass filled with ice. Stir briefly to mix. Slowly pour the half-and-half on top. Garnish with freshly grated nutmeg.

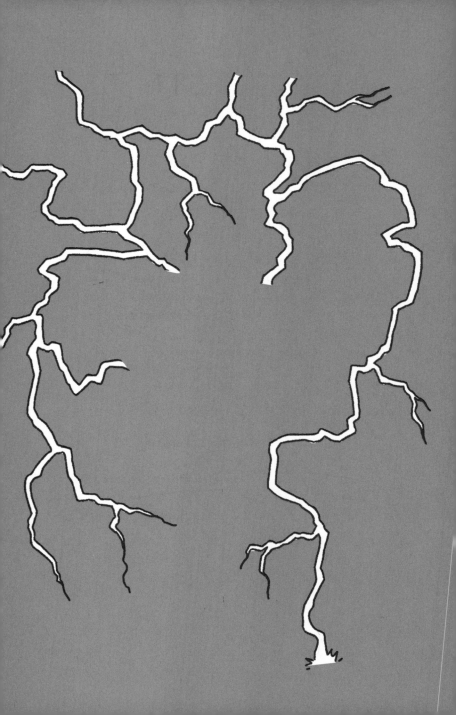

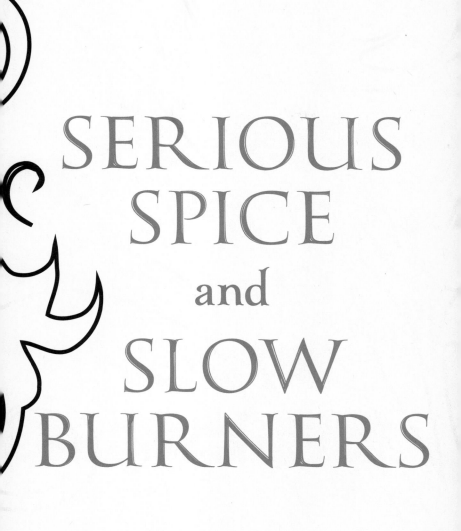

SERIOUS SPICE

and

SLOW BURNERS

BLACK VELVET WING
A Court of Wings and Ruin
by Sarah J. Maas

With Champagne shrouded by Guinness, this cocktail is
just as tall, dark, and handsome as everyone's favorite
sculpted and tattooed hero, Rhysand. The heaviness of
the stout perfectly balances out the glittering tartness of
the Champagne. What better way could there
possibly be to seal a death oath with your
bat-winged High Lord?

Champagne
2½ ounces Guinness

Glassware: Champagne flute

Pour the Champagne, then the stout, carefully into a
chilled Champagne flute. Stir briefly to mix.

LOVE or BURNT MARTINI

SERPENT & DOVE BY SHELBY MAHURIN

You're a witch in hiding, he's a huntsman of the Church; the chemistry is just so hot you think you can smell burning. This Love or Burnt Martini is the perfect sensory cocktail for such a union—the navy-strength gin recalls fireworks, and the Scotch rinse leaves the lingering sensation of smoke. If you're a fan of big smoky flavors, you won't touch another cocktail again.

1 teaspoon smoky Scotch
2 ounces navy-strength gin
½ ounce dry vermouth

Glassware: Martini glass

Pour the Scotch into a martini glass and swirl it around to rinse the glass before tipping out any excess. Fill a mixing glass with ice and add the gin and vermouth. Stir until chilled, then fine-strain into the prepared martini glass. For extra spice, you could add the Scotch to the mixing glass with the gin and vermouth, before stirring.

JULEPS on MINE

A CURSE FOR TRUE LOVE

BY STEPHANIE GARBER

There's nothing more gratifying than a forbidden kiss, but a mint julep might just be the next best thing. It's worth noting that this cocktail is best when you give the mint some time to infuse its tongue-tingling flavor. Waiting may be agony, but you've read two books to get to this point, what's another 10 minutes?

10 to 12 mint leaves
2 ounces bourbon
⅔ ounce simple syrup

Glassware: Julep cup or rocks glass

Add all of the ingredients to your chilled julep cup or rocks glass. Stir gently. If possible leave for 10 minutes or so for the mint to infuse. Add crushed ice and churn with a spoon (preferably a barspoon—the metal disc on one end makes pulling the mint up through the ice super-easy). Top up with more ice and churn again. Finally, cap with ice (in a small mound on top, if you can, for aesthetic reasons), and garnish with a mint sprig or two. You should agitate the mint sprig by slapping it against the back of the hand before placing it into the drink alongside your straw.

GREEDY G&T

A COURT OF SILVER FLAMES BY SARAH J. MAAS

"Greedy," your mate might murmur, as, like Nesta, you want not one, but two . . . kinds of gin in your G&T. Sloe gin would leave you gasping on its own with tonic so the addition of dry gin lightens this cocktail up to but an iridescent mist. Simple and well balanced, it'll go down extremely easily after a long day of training.

1 ounce London dry gin
⅔ ounce sloe gin
Tonic water, to top
1 lemon slice, for garnish
Juniper berries, for garnish

Glassware: Copa de Balon or wine glass

Fill your glass with ice. Add the dry and sloe gins and top with tonic. Stir, then garnish with the lemon slice and a few juniper berries.

DRAGON'S SCALE ALE

FOURTH WING BY REBECCA YARROS

A blend of gin, lemon juice, ginger syrup, and beer, this is a long and refreshing cocktail that pairs perfectly with impenetrable corsets and lightning-hot spice scenes. It's worth taking the time to make your own ginger syrup if you can, as it retains much more of the fiery elements than commercially produced versions. The recipe for the syrup is included below and thankfully doesn't involve any work on the stove, so it'll only be your bedroom at risk of burning down.

1½ ounces gin
1¾ ounces lemon juice
1¾ ounces ginger syrup (see below)
Beer (preferably an ale), to top

Glassware: Pint glass

Add the gin, lemon juice, and ginger syrup to a blender with a couple of ice cubes. Blend until smooth. Fine-strain the mixture into a chilled pint glass. Top with beer.

GINGER SYRUP

In a blender, combine 1 cup plus 1½ teaspoons peeled and chopped fresh root ginger, 1¼ cups superfine sugar, and 4 ounces water and blend until smooth. Fine-strain into a bottle to store until needed.

SPICE and SLOE

THE INADEQUATE HEIR BY DANIELLE L. JENSEN

For when you're really slammed and just need to get to
the good stuff, does anything scream satisfaction more
than spiced sloe gin spilt into apple cider? And like Zarrah
and Keris, if one drink isn't enough for you, feel free to go
again with the warm version. It's guaranteed to heat up
even the coldest of hearts.

Apple cider
2 ounces spiced sloe gin

Glassware: Old-Fashioned glass

Fill your glass with ice. Add the cider, leaving just enough
room at the top for the gin. Gently pour in the sloe gin
over the back of a barspoon to float on top.

You could also drink this as a warm cocktail—add the
cider to a saucepan and put over medium heat. Heat until
the juice is warm (but not boiling) and take off the heat.
Pour the juice into a mug and add the gin.

DRAGON MARGARIDER

IRON FLAME BY REBECCA YARROS

This a cocktail you fight for, that you fly eight hours straight for without even stopping to get your leathers. The key to making it great is using fresh lime juice, squeezed by hand just before it's needed. To get the most out of the fruit, roll it repeatedly against the stone bench of a steamy bathing chamber, or any flat surface you have on hand, before squeezing. Forget dragons, this will be the ride of your life.

1¾ ounces tequila
1 ounce lime juice
1 ounce triple sec or curaçao
1 lime wheel or wedge, for garnish

Glassware: Martini glass

Shake all the ingredients with ice and double-strain into a martini glass with a salted rim. Garnish with the lime wheel or wedge on the side of the glass.

SLOE BURN
THE BRIDGE KINGDOM BY DANIELLE L. JENSEN

The catch with this drink is that it requires a very long
shake, but you'll be rewarded with a delicious, soufflé-like
texture. We know what you're thinking, what's the point
of keeping things light and fluffy? But to truly appreciate
that first sip, you've got to build the tension of the foam;
will it come to a head above the glass, will it simply
overflow? Not everything will be on your terms, but
that's what makes it truly delicious.

2 ounces sloe gin
⅔ ounce whole milk (or use any milk substitute)
½ ounce lemon juice
⅓ ounce lime juice
⅓ ounce simple syrup
1 egg white
1 ounce soda water

Glassware: Highball glass (a straight-sided highball glass will work best)

Fill a cocktail shaker with ice. Add all the ingredients, except for the soda water, and shake for 7 minutes (wrap a kitchen towel around the shaker to stop it getting too cold to hold). It's not necessary to shake nonstop for 7 minutes, just for 7 minutes total. Team up with another person, if possible, to lighten the load. Once shaken, leave the shaker to rest for about 2 minutes.

Open the shaker over the sink so the cocktail doesn't pour out everywhere. Strain the cocktail into the highball glass at the same time as pouring the soda; this will create a fizzy and foamy effect. Fill the glass until about three-quarters full. Put the glass in the fridge for 1 minute, letting the foam settle and get cold. Remove the glass and make a hole in the middle of the foam with a straw. Pour the remaining cocktail into the hole so that the foam rises up the glass. You are aiming to get about a half inch of foam head above the glass.

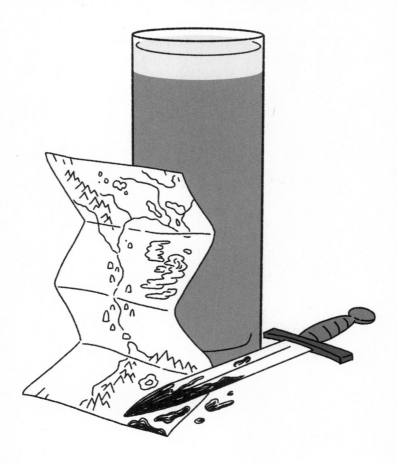

BLOOD and SMUT

FROM *BLOOD AND ASH* BY JENNIFER L. ARMENTROUT

It's no shock that the combination of poppy-red cherry brandy and golden orange juice creates a cocktail guaranteed to make your first night, or perhaps any night, special. Take the following as a warning . . . or a promise: like all the most alluring drinks, it's strictly not for maidens.

1 ounce Scotch
1 ounce sweet vermouth
1 ounce cherry brandy
1 ounce orange juice
1 maraschino cherry, for garnish
1 strip of orange zest, for garnish (optional)

Glassware: Martini glass or Champagne coupe

Add all the ingredients to a cocktail shaker filled with ice. Shake and strain into a chilled martini glass or Champagne coupe.

Garnish with the maraschino cherry or, if you're really fired up, a flambéed piece of orange zest. To flambé the orange zest, first cut a large strip of zest from an orange. Make sure there isn't too much pith on the underside of the zest. Hold it between your fingers, peel-side facing the glass. Take a lighter and hold it between the zest and the drink. In one movement, squeeze the zest to release the oils, which will sparkle in the lighter's flame. Discard the zest and your duties.

HOUSE of HANKY PANKY

HOUSE OF SKY AND BREATH BY SARAH J. MAAS

A sweeter, lighter version of a martini, the House of Hanky Panky is served straight up, which makes it the perfect accompaniment for Maas's breathtaking, straight-to-the-smut sequel. Take a sip and gallop like a gorgeous long-legged faun toward the scene with Ruhn's lip ring; it's less than 100 pages, thank Gods.

1 ounce sweet vermouth
1 ounce gin
2 dashes Fernet-Branca
1 strip of orange zest

Glassware: Martini glass or Champagne coupe

Put all the ingredients into a mixing glass with ice. Stir until well-chilled. Strain into a chilled glass and garnish with the strip of orange zest.

Romantasy Checklist

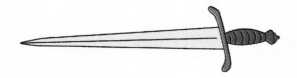

Consider yourself a romantasy connoisseur? Use this list of the most heart-hammering novels to keep track of how many you've read, and how many cocktails you've drunk.

Book	Cocktail
◖ *From Blood and Ash* by Jennifer L. Armentrout	◖ Blood and Smut (p. 141)
◖ *Shadow and Bone* by Leigh Bardugo	◖ Fine, Make Me Your Vesper (p. 33)
◖ *Ninth House* by Leigh Bardugo	◖ Ninth Cocktail (p. 79)
◖ *Hell Bent* by Leigh Bardugo	◖ One Hell of a Sour (p. 117)
◖ *The Familiar* by Leigh Bardugo	◖ Little Scorpion (p. 107)
◖ *The Cruel Prince* by Holly Black	◖ The Cruel Quince Daiquiri (p. 23)
◖ *The Wicked King* by Holly Black	◖ The Wicked Sling (p. 25)
◖ *The Queen of Nothing* by Holly Black	◖ The Kir of Nothing (p. 91)
◖ *One for My Enemy* by Olivie Blake	◖ Magical Manhattan (p. 59)
◖ *The Atlas Six* by Olivie Blake	◖ The Aperol Six (p. 57)
◖ *The Atlas Paradox* by Olivie Blake	◖ Randy Alexandrian (p. 115)
◖ *The Serpent and the Wings of Night* by Carissa Broadbent	◖ Vampiro (p. 27)
◖ *City of Bones* by Cassandra Clare	◖ Mortal Mule (p. 87)

- *The Curse of Saints* by Kate Dramis
- Saints au Champagne (p. 119)
- *Faebound* by Saara El-Arifi
- Bloody Faerie (p. 62)
- *Emily Wilde's Encyclopaedia of Faeries* by Heather Fawcett
- Grumpy Wants Tequila Sunshine (p. 51)
- *Girl, Goddess, Queen* by Bea Fitzgerald
- Girl, Goddess, Gibson (p. 49)
- *The Song of the Marked* by S. M. Gaither
- Brandy Banter (p. 52)
- *Once Upon a Broken Heart* by Stephanie Garber
- Once Upon a Bramble Heart (p. 45)
- *The Ballad of Never After* by Stephanie Garber
- The Ballad of Negroni After (p. 47)
- *A Curse for True Love* by Stephanie Garber
- Juleps on Mine (p. 130)
- *One Dark Window* by Rachel Gillig
- The Devil Within Me (p. 37)
- *These Violent Delights* by Chloe Gong
- Scarlet Collins (p. 94)
- *Our Violent Ends* by Chloe Gong
- A Violent End in the Afternoon (p. 121)
- *Immortal Longings* by Chloe Gong
- Ale of Twin Cities (p. 112)

- ◑ *Belladonna* by Adalyn Grace
- ◑ *The Hurricane Wars* by Thea Guanzon
- ◑ *Bride* by Ali Hazelwood
- ◑ *Bonded by Thorns* by Elizabeth Helen
- ◑ *The Bridge Kingdom* by Danielle L. Jensen
- ◑ *The Inadequate Heir* by Danielle L. Jensen
- ◑ *Godkiller* by Hannah Kaner
- ◑ *Gild* by Raven Kennedy
- ◑ *Throne of Glass* by Sarah J. Maas
- ◑ *A Court of Thorns and Roses* by Sarah J. Maas
- ◑ *A Court of Mist and Fury* by Sarah J. Maas

- ◑ Mourning Glory Fizz (p. 88)
- ◑ You Hit Me Like a Hurricane (p. 74)
- ◑ Old-Fashioned Alpha Male (p. 18)
- ◑ Hair of the Wolf (p. 105)
- ◑ Sloe Burn (p. 138)

- ◑ Spice and Sloe (p. 136)

- ◑ 'Nogkiller (p. 109)
- ◑ White Lies (p. 122)
- ◑ Mai Tai-rant (p. 31)

- ◑ She's Got a Concealed Weapon (p. 40)

- ◑ A Coupe of Thorns and Rose (p. 85)
- ◑ Green-Eyed Faerie (p. 35)

- ◑ High Lady (p. 69)

- *A Court of Wings and Ruin* by Sarah J. Maas
- Black Velvet Wing (p. 127)
- *A Court of Frost and Starlight* by Sarah J. Maas
- A Twinkle of Frost and Starlight (p. 101)
- *A Court of Silver Flames* by Sarah J. Maas
- Greedy G&T (p. 133)
- *House of Earth and Blood* by Sarah J. Maas
- Crescent City Cosmopolitan (p. 71)
- *House of Sky and Breath* by Sarah J. Maas
- House of Hanky Panky (p. 143)
- *House of Flame and Shadow* by Sarah J. Maas
- Flame House Punch (p. 73)
- *Shatter Me* by Tahereh Mafi
- Smash Me (p. 65)
- *This Woven Kingdom* by Tahereh Mafi
- Pine After Colada (p. 77)
- *Serpent & Dove* by Shelby Mahurin
- Love or Burnt Martini (p. 129)
- *A Marvellous Light* by Freya Marske
- A Marvellous, Light Lemonade (p. 99)
- *Ledge* by Stacey McEwan
- Beast Between the Sheets (p. 29)

- *Zodiac Academy: The Awakening* by Caroline Peckham and Susanne Valenti
- Shape-Shifter Spritz (p. 89)

- *Where the Dark Stands Still* by A. B. Poranek
- Cursed Forest Mojito (p. 81)

- *Neon Gods* by Katee Robert
- Ambrosia (p. 93)

- *Hunt on Dark Waters* by Katee Robert
- Hunt Me on Dark and Stormy Waters (p. 96)

- *Powerless* by Lauren Roberts
- Viscous Little Thing (p. 43)

- *The Priory of the Orange Tree* by Samantha Shannon
- The Priory of the Orange-tini (p. 67)

- *A Court This Cruel and Lovely* by Stacia Stark
- Morally Greyhound (p. 20)

- *Fourth Wing* by Rebecca Yarros
- The Gauntlet Gimlet (p. 55)
- Dragon's Scale Ale (p. 134)

- *Iron Flame* by Rebecca Yarros
- Empyrean Espresso Martini (p. 111)
- Dragon Margarider (p. 137)

Credits

WHAT TO SERVE YOUR SHADOW KING

Bride by Ali Hazelwood, Little, Brown Book Group, 2024

A Court This Cruel and Lovely by Stacia Stark, Bingeable Books LLC, 2023

The Cruel Prince by Holly Black, Hot Key Books, 2018

The Wicked King by Holly Black, Hot Key Books, 2019

The Serpent and the Wings of Night by Carissa Broadbent, Tor Publishing Group, 2023

Ledge by Stacey McEwan, Angry Robot Books, 2022

Gild by Raven Kennedy, Penguin Books, 2020

Shadow and Bone by Leigh Bardugo, Indigo, 2012

A Court of Thorns and Roses by Sarah J. Maas, Bloomsbury, 2015

One Dark Window by Rachel Gillig, Bloomsbury, 2022

A TOAST TO BITTER RIVALS

Throne of Glass by Sarah J. Maas, Bloomsbury, 2012

Powerless by Lauren Roberts, Simon & Schuster, 2023

Once Upon a Broken Heart by Stephanie Garber, Hodder & Stoughton, 2021

The Ballad of Never After by Stephanie Garber, Hodder & Stoughton, 2022

Girl, Goddess, Queen by Bea Fitzgerald, Penguin Books, 2023

Emily Wilde's Encyclopaedia of Faeries by Heather Fawcett, Little, Brown Book Group, 2023

The Song of the Marked by S. M. Gaither, Yellow Door Publishing INC, 2020

Fourth Wing by Rebecca Yarros, Little, Brown Group, 2023

The Atlas Six by Olivie Blake, Tor Publishing Group, 2022

One for My Enemy by Olivie Blake, Tor Publishing Group, 2023

FRUITS OF THE FAE

Faebound by Saara El-Arifi, HarperCollins Publishers, 2024

Shatter Me by Tahereh Mafi, Electric Monkey, 2018

The Priory of the Orange Tree by Samantha Shannon, Bloomsbury, 2019

A Court of Mist and Fury by Sarah J. Maas, Bloomsbury, 2016

House of Earth and Blood by Sarah J. Maas, Bloomsbury, 2020

House of Flame and Shadow by Sarah J. Maas, Bloomsbury, 2024

The Hurricane Wars by Thea Guanzon, HarperCollins Publishers, 2023

This Woven Kingdom by Tahereh Mafi, HarperCollins Publishers, 2022

Ninth House by Leigh Bardugo, Gollancz, 2019

Where the Dark Stands Still by A. B. Poranek, Penguin Books, 2024

SCRUMPTIOUS SPRITZES

A Court of Thorns and Roses by Sarah J. Maas, Bloomsbury, 2015

City of Bones by Cassandra Clare, Walker Books, 2007

Belladonna by Adalyn Grace, Hodder & Stoughton, 2022

Zodiac Academy: The Awakening by Caroline Peckham and Susanne Valenti, self-published, 2019

The Queen of Nothing by Holly Black, Hot Key Books, 2019

Neon Gods by Katee Robert, SourceBooks, 2021

These Violent Delights by Chloe Gong, Hodder & Stoughton, 2020

Hunt on Dark Waters by Katee Robert, Del Rey, 2023

A Marvellous Light by Freya Marske, Tor Publishing Group, 2021

A Court of Frost and Starlight by Sarah J. Maas, Bloomsbury, 2018

TOE-CURLING TIPPLES

Bonded by Thorns by Elizabeth Helen, Luna Fox Press, 2023

The Familiar by Leigh Bardugo, Penguin Books, 2024

Godkiller by Hannah Kaner, HarperCollins Publishers, 2023

Iron Flame by Rebecca Yarros, Little, Brown Group, 2023

Immortal Longings by Chloe Gong, Hodder & Stoughton, 2023

The Atlas Paradox by Olivie Blake, Tor Publishing Group, 2022

Hell Bent by Leigh Bardugo, Gollancz, 2023

The Curse of Saints by Kate Dramis, Michael Joseph, 2023

Our Violent Ends by Chloe Gong, Hodder & Stoughton, 2020

SERIOUS SPICE AND SLOW BURNERS

A Court of Wings and Ruin by Sarah J. Maas, Bloomsbury, 2017

Serpent & Dove by Shelby Mahurin, HarperCollins Publishers, 2019

A Curse for True Love by Stephanie Garber, Hodder & Stoughton, 2023

A Court of Silver Flames by Sarah J. Maas, Bloomsbury, 2021

Fourth Wing by Rebecca Yarros, Little, Brown Group, 2023

The Inadequate Heir by Danielle L. Jensen, Penguin Books, 2022

Iron Flame by Rebecca Yarros, Little, Brown Group, 2023

The Bridge Kingdom by Danielle L. Jensen, Penguin Books, 2022

From Blood and Ash by Jennifer L. Armentrout, Blue Box Press, 2020

House of Sky and Breath by Sarah J. Maas, Bloomsbury, 2022

This or That

W hat are your romantasy preferences? Answer these alone or share it with your book club (perhaps with a delicious drink in hand) to find out . . .

This	**That**
◑ *Fated Mates*	◑ Enemies to Lovers
◑ *Forbidden Love*	◑ Cross-Species
◑ *Love Triangles*	◑ Secret Identity
◑ *Grumpy*	◑ Sunshine
◑ *True Love's Kiss*	◑ Reluctant Companions
◑ *Alpha Male*	◑ Shadow King
◑ *Girl Boss*	◑ Crusader
◑ *Forced Proximity*	◑ Found Family
◑ *Resurrection*	◑ Transformation

Index

Published in the United States by Clarkson Potter/Publishers,
an imprint of the Crown Publishing Group, a division of
Penguin Random House LLC, New York.
ClarksonPotter.com

CLARKSON POTTER is a trademark and POTTER with colophon
is a registered trademark of Penguin Random House LLC.

Library of Congress Cataloging-in-Publication Data
is on file with the publisher.

ISBN 979-8-217-03386-7
Ebook ISBN 979-8-217-03387-4

Printed in the United States of America on acid-free paper.

Clarkson Potter/Publishers Team, New York
Editor: Jennifer Sit | Editorial assistant: Elaine Hennig
Contributing Designer: Yasmeen Bandoo
Production editors: Terry Deal and Taylor Teague
Production manager: Jessica Heim
Compositor: North Market Street Graphics and Hannah Hunt
Proofreader: Tess Rossi | Indexer: Ken DellaPenta
Marketer: Paola Crespo

Ebury Press Team, London
Writer: Alice Johnstone
Illustrator: Ollie Mann
Designer: Francesca Corsini

1st Printing

First US Edition